A Gift for

_____

From

_____

Date

_____

Visit Tyndale's exciting Web site at www.tyndale.com

Whisper a Prayer

Copyright © 2004 by Mark Gilroy Communications, Inc.

Designed by Beth Sparkman

Photography credits:
Pages: 18, 20, 22, 40-42, 50, 56-57, 60, 64, 72, 76, 88-90, 92 © by Michael Hudson;
Pages: 10, 30, 34, 36, 46, 68 © by Photodisc; Page: 78 © by Digital Vision; Pages: 16, 17,
24, 26, 32, 54, 62-63, 67, 84, 86 © by Image State; Page: 94 © by Brand X; Pages: 6, 8, 44,
56-57, 94 © by Photos.com. All rights reserved.

ISBN 0-8423-8293-3

Printed in Italy

09 08 07 06 05 04
6 5 4 3 2 1

grant me peace

Whisper a Prayer

Pray

TYNDALE HOUSE PUBLISHERS, INC.
WHEATON, ILLINOIS

Enter into His gates with thanksgiving,

And into His courts with praise.

Be thankful to Him,

and bless His name.

Psalm 100:4, NKJV

Introduction

You are invited into the presence of the one true God, creator of the universe, the One who knows you best and loves you most . . . even though you are entering his royal courts, he does not call for pomp and circumstance. He wants you to visit him with singing, dancing, joy, praise, a deep sense of trust, and thanksgiving.

Nothing will touch your spirit and change your outlook on life more profoundly than when you know there is a God who cares about you and hears your prayers. Peace replaces worry. Courage replaces fear. A sense of direction replaces confusion. Comfort washes over your pain.

Alone or in a crowd, whether your need seems great or small, bring all your worries, all your needs, all your worship—all your life—to God. He will hear even the faintest of whispers.

Are you ready to experience God's wonderful peace? Simply whisper a prayer.

My voice You shall hear in the morning, O Lord.

Psalm 5:3, NKJV

You Hear Me

O Lord,

Thank you that you really do hear me when I call out to you. There are so many others who promise to always be there, but no one else is as faithful and true as you are. Others try their best to understand my words, but only you know my heart.

I am filled with gratitude at the thought that you listen, that you have infinite patience, and that you care to hear my thoughts as I bring my needs and praise before you.

Lord, I know this is no burden to you. You want me to bring my cares and all of my life before you. And so I promise you that you will hear my voice in the morning.

affirm one another

Let us consider how we may spur one another

on toward love and good deeds.

Hebrews 10:24, NIV

Words of Encouragement

Heavenly Father,

You have created us to affirm one another and to be a blessing to our families, communities, and the entire world.

I think of my closest friends. Father, I ask that you give me words of encouragement for each one of them. Help me to fan the flames of their faith in you. Help me to gently remind them that they were created by you for love and good deeds.

You alone empower us to accomplish your will in the world, but I am humbled—and excited—to know that you can use even me to bring about your plans.

Celebrate! Worship and recommit to God!

Nahum 1:15, *THE MESSAGE*

Celebrate!

Heavenly Father,

You have not created and redeemed me to live a dull, gray, joyless, plodding life. Oh yes, I know you want me to be sober minded, to be true to my vows, but you don't want me to take my life or myself so seriously that joy and laughter are squeezed from my soul.

Thank you for creating a world filled with wonder and delight. Thank you for family and friends that make my life so rich. Thank you that you want me to find pleasure in following your will and ways.

I am so thankful and blessed to join the celebration you have created for our enjoyment.

I strain to reach the end of the race and receive

the prize for which God, through Christ Jesus,

is calling us up to heaven.

Philippians 3:14, NLT

The Prize

Heavenly Father,

There is so much I want to accomplish. You know my dreams and goals. Some of these aspirations are noble and worthy; others, I confess, are superficial and spring out of my own selfishness.

Thank you, O God, for those dreams and goals that you have planted in my heart—and for giving me the wisdom to know which ones matter most. Help me to pursue them with your strength and direction.

Even more importantly, Father, help me to always press toward the greatest goal and greatest prize of all—to love you with all my heart. When I get caught up in my own plans, remind me through the Holy Spirit that the greatest prize of all is knowing you!

Do not forget to do good and to share with others, for with such sacrifices God is pleased.

Hebrews 13:16, NIV

Pleasing God

Merciful God,

You are an awesome God, full of compassion and kindness. Your love and mercy know no bounds. Your heart is always turned toward those who are hurting and who have serious needs.

I really want to do good deeds and reach out to others, but sometimes I get so caught up in my own life that I forget to act. I ask that you renew in me a heart of compassion and give me the strength to do something about it.

As I share with the needy, I will also remember to praise you for the many blessings you have given me.

I have hidden your word in my heart that I might not sin against you.

Psalm 119:11, NIV

Hidden in My Heart

O Lord,

You know that I want to live with honesty and integrity before you. When some who claim the name of Jesus fall into sin, I have seen how it undermines the confidence of other Christians and brings dishonor to your name.

I don't want to be a hypocrite, claiming to be holy while practicing all kinds of sin. I know that I am not perfect and that you are always ready to forgive and restore me if I fall. But I ask you for the power to live a life of honor.

I will hide your Word in my heart today—and every day—so that I will stand strong against temptation!

But as for me, it is good to be near God.

Psalm 73:28, NIV

Near to You

My God,

I don't want to build my self-esteem on the basis of material possessions or personal accomplishments—or even on the blessings of cherished friends and family members.

I affirm that knowing you is my ultimate source of hope, joy, love, faith, confidence, success, and every other blessing. Since you came into my heart, my life has never been the same.

So no matter how tough the challenges I face or how great the joys I experience, I declare that, for me, it is so good just to be near you, O God.

He has remembered His mercy and His

faithfulness to the house of Israel.

Psalm 98:3, NKJV

You Remember

Dear Lord,

You remembered Moses, who toiled in a desert exile for forty years, and made him the leader of a new nation.

You remembered Hannah, who grieved that she was unable to bear a child, and gave her a son called Samuel.

You remembered David, who was hunted like a wild animal to be killed, and gave him the throne of Israel.

You remembered Paul, who was a stubborn and hateful religious persecutor, and gave him a vision of Jesus that forever changed his life.

And I thank you, O Lord, that no matter what the circumstances of my life, you remember me!

The Lord is my shepherd, I shall not be in want.

He makes me lie down in green pastures,

he leads me beside quiet waters,

he restores my soul.

Psalm 23:1-2, NIV

Green Pastures

My Shepherd,

It is so wonderful to stop each day to spend time alone with you in prayer and in your Word. You are such a good shepherd, who knows when I need rest, when I need to pull away from the noises of life to experience peace and quiet.

My Shepherd, please remind me when I need to turn off the radio or television or stop looking at a computer screen. Remind me that the deepest need of my life is not any material possession I don't have, but to be close to you—for then everything else takes care of itself.

Thank you for green pastures and quiet waters.

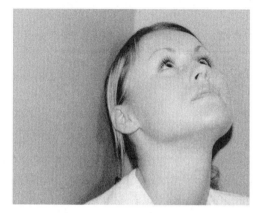

May the words of my mouth and the
thoughts of my heart be pleasing to you,
O Lord, my rock and my redeemer.

Psalm 19:14, NLT

peace, faith, optimism
AND love

My Words

Merciful God,

You know the many times when I have not guarded my thoughts or been careful with my words. I have harbored anger and resentment. I have expressed sarcasm and malice.

O merciful God, forgive me for not reflecting your kindness and grace, for not seeking to please you at all times in my thoughts and words.

Thank you for being my rock, for truly being my source of strength. You enable me to do things that I cannot do with my own efforts and intentions. And so today, I look forward to thinking about what is noble and true; I look forward to speaking words of peace, faith, optimism, and love to the people I encounter.

Seek his will in all you do,

and he will direct your paths.

Proverbs 3:6, NLT

Direct My Paths

Trustworthy God,

You know the times when I strayed onto paths that you didn't want me to take. I am sorry for my carelessness and my stubbornness, for those times when I just didn't have the faith to believe that you always know what's best for me.

Thank you, God, for guiding me back onto the right paths for my life through your patience and love.

I acknowledge that you alone are completely trustworthy, that you alone are all-knowing. And so it is with confidence and gratitude that I commit all the areas of my life to you. Show me your will and guide my steps today.

I will put My law in their minds,

and write it on their hearts.

Jeremiah 31:33, NKJV

A New Heart

Gracious Father,

I don't want my relationship with you to be based on rules, regulations, or a mere sense of duty. And I know that is not the kind of relationship you want with me.

I am so glad that you desire a spontaneous, joyful, growing union with me. I am truly amazed that you have put what you want and expect of me inside my mind and upon my heart.

In a world that does not always know right from wrong, I turn to your Word with a renewed heart and mind as I seek to follow your ways in all that I do.

Weeping may endure for a night,

But joy comes in the morning.

Psalm 30:5, NKJV

JOY

Joy Comes in the Morning

God of Comfort,

When my heart is filled with sorrow, it is so easy to let discouragement dominate my spirit.

I forget that you are at work on my behalf, even in my toughest and most painful moments. Most importantly, you are at work in my life, making me into the person you want me to become.

This morning is a wonderful reminder that you are a God of healing and renewal. Thank you so much for giving me a new sense of joy and a new perspective on life.

Give thanks to the Lord, for he is good;

his love endures forever.

Psalm 107:1, NIV

Thank You

Dear Lord,

Because of your Spirit within me, I am a person of gratitude! I refuse to take my blessings for granted. I refuse to complain about petty annoyances and inconveniences. I refuse to focus on what I don't have when I live in a land of plenty. I refuse to grumble and gossip when there is so much positive to see and say.

Today, Lord, I say thank you, thank you, thank you, thank you! And I'm not going to stop there. I plan to tell others how grateful I am for your goodness and your love that endures forever.

Even as I say thank you, I receive so much in return as my soul is renewed and my whole outlook on life is lifted.

Oh, the joys of those who do not follow the advice of the wicked, or stand around with sinners, or join in with scoffers. But they delight in doing everything the Lord wants; day and night they think about his law. They are like trees planted along the riverbank, bearing fruit each season without fail. Their leaves never wither, and in all they do, they prosper.

Psalm 1:1-3, NLT

Bearing Fruit

Dear Lord,

I know that you want us to love all people, but I ask you to help me steer clear of those people who would drag down my spirit and undermine my faith because of their cynicism and wickedness.

I draw renewal from your river of grace, O Lord. And I pray that I will be a positive influence in the life of every person I know. Help my words to exhibit a delight in following you.

Thank you for making me faithful and fruitful—not just some of the time, but in every season and situation.

Be silent, and know that I am God!

Psalm 46:10, NLT

Know that
I am God

Be Silent

Dear God,

When I am in your presence, there are no awkward pauses. I am not judged by whether I have all the right words to say. Your Spirit speaks on my behalf when I can't express my thoughts as clearly as I would like.

And just as you invite me to voice all my worries and needs to you, you bid me to come silently before you so that I can realize again how awesome you are; so that I can hear your voice as you speak to me with encouragement, direction, and correction; so that I can feel the spiritual intimacy of just being close to you.

Today, I will praise you audibly with my lips— and silently with my heart.

Serve the Lord with gladness,

Come before His presence with singing.

Psalm 100:2, NKJV

Gladly Serving

Lord,

When I am tempted to ignore those around me who are hurting because I don't feel like I have enough energy—and I'd rather get on with my own plans—would you remind me again of the strength and joy that you fill me with when I obey you?

It is no burden or chore to serve you, O Lord. It is a privilege and a joy. I know that it is a source of supernatural empowerment.

I will serve you—and those you love so much—with gladness and a song in my heart.

Dear brothers and sisters, I plead with you to give your bodies to God. Let them be a living and holy sacrifice—the kind he will accept. When you think of what he has done for you, is this too much to ask? Don't copy the behavior and customs of this world, but let God transform you into a new person by changing the way you think. Then you will know what God wants you to do, and you will know how good and pleasing and perfect his will really is.

Romans 12:1-2, NLT

His Perfect Will

Dear God,

Today I renew my commitment to you. I am totally yours—all of me. Because of your unbelievable mercy toward me, I offer myself as a living sacrifice to you.

I don't want to be a conformist, just drifting along and copying the patterns of this world. I want to be different in the ways that truly make a difference, even when it means swimming against popular currents. I pray that you will continue to transform me into a person who pleases you.

And renew my mind, O God, that I may know your good, pleasing, and perfect will for my life!

*Dear brothers and sisters, let me say one more
thing as I close this letter. Fix your thoughts
on what is true and honorable and right.
Think about things that are pure and lovely
and admirable. Think about things that are
excellent and worthy of praise.*

Philippians 4:8, NLT

Things of Excellence

Dear God,

The world is filled with crude, profane, crass, and negative images and sounds. Sometimes they are wrapped up so invitingly, it is almost impossible not to watch, listen, and laugh.

I want my soul to be stirred by what is true, honorable, and right. I want my spirit to bask in those things that are lovely, admirable, excellent, and worthy of praise. When I am bombarded by the profane, I pray that you would give me the sensitivity and willpower to turn away.

Thank you for lifting my eyes and my spirit to the beautiful and excellent gifts you have placed before me.

Do everything without complaining
or arguing, so that you may become blameless
and pure, children of God without fault in a
crooked and depraved generation, in which
you shine like stars in the universe.

Philippians 2:14-15, NIV

Shine like Stars

God of Peace,

It is so easy to fall into the habit of griping and bickering. I am embarrassed when I think of some of the arguments I've had. I'm ashamed when I remember times I've complained, when I have so many blessings from you.

I don't want to follow the patterns of strife that are so prevalent in our world. I want to stand pure and blameless, even if others around me are deceitful and practice all kinds of evil.

I want to reflect your love and purity in my words and spirit. I pray that today I will shine like a star in the night sky.

The Lord said to Samuel, "Don't judge by his
appearance or height, for I have rejected him.
The Lord doesn't make decisions the way you
do! People judge by outward appearance, but
the Lord looks at a person's thoughts and
intentions."

1 Samuel 16:7, NLT

Outward Appearances

O Lord,

You know how insecure I am when I believe that I don't measure up to others. And Lord, I know how superficial and shallow I've been when judging others based solely on appearances.

You look at the heart, at our thoughts and intentions. You don't turn away from any because of their clothing or their looks. Will you give me the eyes to see others with the same openness and compassion that you do?

Lord, though you tell us that physical training and exercise are of some value, though you want us to present ourselves with respect, help me to keep my focus on first being a person of beauty on the inside.

Watch out! Be very careful never to forget
what you have seen the Lord do for you. Do
not let these things escape from your mind as
long as you live! And be sure to pass them on
to your children and grandchildren.

Deuteronomy 4:9, NLT

I Won't Forget!

Dear Lord,

Oh, how easy it is to forget all you have done in my life. When I face challenges, I am tempted to be fearful and complain about my lot in life. When everything is going great, I am tempted to take all the credit and not acknowledge my need of you.

Give me a spirit of remembering. Help me to remember your mighty deeds throughout history. You are truly a God of miracles and redemption.

Help me always remember what you have done in my life—and to share my story with others so that they would open their hearts to you.

The eternal God is your refuge,

and his everlasting arms are under you.

Deuteronomy 33:27, NLT

A Safe Haven

Eternal God,

Truly you are my refuge when I feel threatened because there are evil people in the world who would harm me if they had opportunity.

Rather than live in fear, I take comfort and gain confidence in the knowledge that you wrap your arms of love and protection around me.

Make me wise, O God, so that I do my part to carefully avoid dangerous situations. Thank you for the times you have protected me when I didn't even know I was in danger, and for the times you will protect me in the future.

EVERLASTING ARMS

O Lord, you are so good, so ready to
forgive, so full of unfailing love for all who ask
your aid.

Psalm 86:5, NLT

Unfailing Love

Dear Lord,

So many times I don't receive what I need from you simply because I fail to ask for your help. But you invite me to bring every care and concern that I have and come boldly before you.

Today I ask for your help for a relationship problem you know about, for a situation that needs your intervention concerning a friend, for the grace and strength to forgive others just as you have forgiven me.

You are a good God. Help me to express that same goodness, forgiveness, and love to the people in my life.

I love the Lord because he hears

and answers my prayers.

Because he bends down and listens,

I will pray as long as I have breath!

Psalm 116:1-2, NLT

As Long As I Have Breath!

Gracious Lord,

I never knew how much grace, comfort, and joy I could experience simply by talking to you in prayer each day. Prayer has become so real to me. It's no longer a mere block of time, but an ongoing conversation throughout my day.

I don't ever want to go back to living solely off my own resources, not remembering that you are always present to hear and answer my prayers. You have bent down near to me and allowed me to glimpse your presence in my life.

So with all my breath, I will express my worship, my gratitude, and my needs to you.

You are worthy, O Lord our God, to receive glory and honor and power. For you created everything, and it is for your pleasure that they exist and were created.

Revelation 4:11, NLT

You Are Worthy

O Lord My God,

Free me from the self-centeredness and arrogance of a world that does not acknowledge you as creator and sustainer of all that exists. You have given us so many good gifts—a beautiful world, intelligence and reason, free will, and so much more—that we have claimed these blessings and powers as our own.

I was created to please you, O Lord, and I want to do that in all areas of my life—my thoughts, my speech, my relationships, my generosity, my compassion, my kindness.

In all that I do, I acknowledge your greatness . . . for you alone are worthy of my praise.

57

If we confess our sins to him, he is faithful and just to forgive us and to cleanse us from every wrong.

1 John 1:9, NLT

Forgive Me

Dear God,

I don't want anything to come between you and me in our relationship.

I come before you today with humbleness, knowing the things I have done wrong out of anger and carelessness and pride. I also come with the assurance that you want me to be open and completely honest with you about my life, even the areas where I feel shame. I am amazed at your grace, for you know everything about me, yet you still want me to draw near to you.

God, I confess my sins to you right now. Thank you for the peace and freedom that are mine as you touch my heart and make me clean again.

My God shall supply all your need according

to His riches in glory by Christ Jesus.

Philippians 4:19, NKJV

All My Needs

O God,

I don't want to allow fear and worry to dominate my life. But you know the concern I feel about my finances right now.

I ask that you would grant me the grace not to permit fear to rob me of joy, not to let worry come between me and the people I love, not to allow legitimate concerns to undermine my faith and optimism.

Show me ways in which I can grow in my responsibility toward finances. Guide my steps toward financial success and freedom. I live in complete confidence that whether I have little or much at this moment, you meet my every need.

The Lord says, "I will guide you along the best pathway for your life. I will advise you and watch over you."

Psalm 32:8, NLT

I LISTEN

What Should I Do?

Lord,

You know that I want to please you, to serve you, to follow your will for my life. But sometimes I don't know how best to do that.

Lord, I need your counsel right now. I know there are many good activities I could pursue, many excellent paths I could follow. Would you show me the *best* path for my life? I don't want to look back on my life with regret because I didn't accomplish what you most wanted me to do.

Thank you that you promise to guide me and watch over my life. I know you are quietly speaking to me even now. Help my heart to be open and receptive and faithful as I listen for your voice today.

OR YOUR VOICE

He was wounded for our transgressions,

He was bruised for our iniquities;

The chastisement for our peace was upon Him,

And by His stripes we are healed.

Isaiah 53:5, NKJV

By His Stripes

Lord,

How easy it is for me to blame others for the problems of the world. How tempting it is to proclaim my innocence and refuse to accept responsibility for my actions.

You gently remind me that everyone has sinned and gone astray—my life has not been blameless. Everyone is deserving of punishment, including me.

And yet you gave your Son to pay the price for my transgressions. O Lord, I will thank you all of my days as I receive with profound gratitude the salvation, the peace, the restoration, and the healing that are mine through the suffering and blood of Jesus.

Praise the name of God forever and ever,

for he alone has all wisdom and power.

He determines the course of world events;

he removes kings and sets others on the throne.

Daniel 2:20, NLT

You Are in Control

Eternal, All-Powerful God,

When I open a newspaper or turn on the television, I am bombarded with reports of war, murder, strife, abuse, robbery, corruption, and terrorism. My soul becomes heavy. I begin to lose heart.

Then I am reminded that you are ultimately in control of the world. I have nothing to fear, for you will not forsake those who love you. Even though evil persons are allowed to act for a season, a day is fast approaching when peace and righteousness will prevail.

I pray that your will be done on earth as it is in heaven, believing fully that it will be so. And I praise your name, O God, today and forever!

"Don't sin by letting anger gain control over you." Don't let the sun go down while you are still angry, for anger gives a mighty foothold to the Devil.

Ephesians 4:26-27, NLT

Anger

Heavenly Father,

You know how easy it is for me to flash in anger. I know that anger is a natural human emotion that doesn't have to lead to sin, but I never want to damage my relationships or weaken my spiritual life by letting anger control me.

I ask, heavenly Father, that you would help me to be much slower to anger than I am now; to not lash out at others with harsh and angry words—and if I ever do, to seek their forgiveness immediately; to be quick to forgive; to refuse to give the devil a foothold in my life by harboring anger overnight.

Father, thank you for making me a person of self-control and poise.

quick to forgive

I can do all things through Christ who strengthens me.

Philippians 4:13, NKJV

I Feel Inadequate

Mighty God,

You have promised not to allow challenges, burdens, or temptations to come my way without also providing me the strength to handle them.

But I confess that there are times when I haven't been strong enough to triumph over the circumstances I have faced. I've not exhibited the poise and grace that should characterize my life. And when I look at people around me who seem to have everything together, my sense of inadequacy is heightened.

What amazes me is that when I confess my lack of power and how much I really need you, you step in to do for me what I cannot do myself. Dear God, today I declare that you are my true source of strength. By faith I declare that I can do all things because you make me more than adequate for my tasks.

His compassions never fail.

They are new every morning.

Lamentations 3:22-23, NIV

New Each Morning

Compassionate Lord,

You promise to give me new mercies every single morning of my life. I don't have to store up grace, mercy, or faith from yesterday. Your fresh touch on my life is up-to-date every moment of every day.

I receive your mercies today with a deep sense of gratitude and appreciation—knowing full well how much I need them. And whether my days are tough or easy, I don't ever want to take this gift from you lightly or for granted.

I will rejoice and give you praise, O Lord, for the tender mercies that are mine for knowing and trusting you.

Well done, my good and faithful servant. You have been faithful in handling this small amount, so now I will give you many more responsibilities. Let's celebrate together!

Matthew 25:21, NLT

Opportunities and Challenges

Dear Faithful Father,

I lay my heart and life before you today. Continue to transform me into a person of great character and faithfulness. I want to please you in every situation, great or small. Give me strength and courage to . . .

◆ not participate when others are gossiping,

◆ flee when temptation comes my way,

◆ speak up when I have an opportunity to tell someone about your goodness,

◆ defend the one who is being mistreated,

◆ forgive someone who has offended me, even when I know it won't be reciprocated,

◆ accept an opportunity to minister, even though it takes me outside my comfort zone.

Father, help me to be ever faithful with the gifts you have given me.

Peace I leave with you, My peace I give to you, not as the world gives do I give to you. Let not your heart be troubled, neither let it be afraid.

John 14:27, NKJV

I Feel Stressed

Dear God,

Right now my life does not feel very together. Tasks are undone. I'm struggling with some big decisions. I'm not as connected to my friends and loved ones as I want to be. I seemingly can't get anywhere on time.

I confess that my confidence is low right now due to the stress I'm feeling. But I still cling to the promise of Jesus that he will grant me peace. Lord, take my meager offering of faith and help it to blossom into something beautiful in my heart today.

Because of your presence, I let go of my troubles and fears; I accept your gracious offer of peace with a thankful heart.

You will live in joy and peace. The mountains and hills will burst into song, and the trees of the field will clap their hands!

Isaiah 55:12, NLT

A New Song

God of Peace,

Thank you for creating me to experience peace, joy, and happiness. Oh, you want me to be sober, respectful, caring, and serious minded, but you also invite me to celebrate, smile, and laugh at the goodness and wonder of the world you have created.

Today I remember that you are God—and you have the world under control. I'm not going to worry, judge, or walk around with a scowl on my face. I'm going to join the mountains, trees, and all your creation in worship by making a joyful noise, clapping my hands, and singing a song of praise to you.

I ask that you would allow the people I encounter today to see that you are a God of peace and joy because of my new song.

Remember this—a farmer who plants only a few seeds will get a small crop. But the one who plants generously will get a generous crop. You must each make up your own mind as to how much you should give. Don't give reluctantly or in response to pressure. For God loves the person who gives cheerfully. And God will generously provide all you need. Then you will always have everything you need and plenty left over to share with others.

2 Corinthians 9:6-8, NLT

A Cheerful Giver

O Generous God,

You have blessed me in so many ways. I live in a land of plenty. Even when I face tough times financially, you provide me with food, clothing, and shelter. You have given me everything I need, with plenty left over to share.

I pray that through the Holy Spirit you would fan into flame the seed of generosity in my heart. I don't want to be stingy. I don't want to pinch pennies with others when what you have given me is so much greater.

Open my eyes to the needs around me and throughout the world. Open my heart that I would cheerfully and generously bless the lives of others through offerings of love.

Let us not grow weary while doing good, for in due season we shall reap if we do not lose heart.

Galatians 6:9, NKJV

I Won't Quit!

Dear Lord,

Even if friends or family forsake me . . . I won't quit!

Even if someone I admire greatly should fall . . . I won't quit!

Even if someone I forgive won't be reconciled . . . I won't quit!

Even if I should become sick or face other trials . . . I won't quit!

Even if my church experiences problems and strife . . . I won't quit!

Even if my life doesn't measure up to what you expect from me and what I expect from myself. . . I won't quit!

You have helped me plant seeds of faith and grace in my life and in others' lives through my deeds. You have promised that if I don't quit, there will be a great harvest in the proper season.

Lord, I'm not quitting now!

STRONG

A final word: Be strong with the Lord's mighty power. Put on all of God's armor so that you will be able to stand firm against all strategies and tricks of the Devil.

Ephesians 6:10-11, NLT

Standing Firm

Dear Lord,

I sometimes forget that there is someone who wants nothing more than to lure me down wrong paths and separate me from a vital relationship with you.

Make me vigilant so that I will be on guard against the strategies and tricks the devil uses against me. One moment he is like a roaring lion trying to strike fear in my heart. The next moment he is like an angel of light trying to seduce me into doing what is wrong.

Thank you that this battle is not mine to fight alone. You give me every weapon and item of armor I need to stand strong: truth, faith, salvation, peace, the Word, and the Holy Spirit. Thank you for giving me the strength to be victorious against Satan's attacks.

Dear brothers and sisters, if another Christian

is overcome by some sin, you who are godly

should gently and humbly help that person

back onto the right path. And be careful not to

fall into the same temptation yourself.

Galatians 6:1, NLT

A Prayer for My Friends

Redeemer God,

You know my friends who are struggling against sin—and losing. I have seen these friends walk closely with you, and it hurts to watch them stray from your paths and protection.

I offer my faith and my prayers on their behalf right now. You are a kind and gracious God, quick to forgive our sins when we confess them. Please send your Holy Spirit to convict and convince them of their need to be restored in their relationship with you.

Give me words of insight to help and not alienate. And keep me safe from any temptation that is alive and at work in their lives right now.

There is therefore now no condemnation to those who are in Christ Jesus, who do not walk according to the flesh, but according to the Spirit.

Romans 8:1, NKJV

Not Guilty

Dear God,

When I was lost and without you, I heard you call out
to me with words of mercy, forgiveness, and healing.
I will never forget the moment that I first believed
that my life was empty without you.

Before, I had always lived in the flesh, relying
solely on my own thoughts, my own wants, and my
own strength. Then the Holy Spirit came to dwell
in my heart, and a whole new world opened before
me. I discovered a dimension of life—my spiritual
nature—which I had only suspected before.

God, when my own thoughts or the words of
others condemn me, remind me in my spirit that I am
united with Jesus Christ, and that he offers life, not death.

*Consequently, you are no longer foreigners
and aliens, but fellow citizens with God's
people and members of God's household.*

Ephesians 2:19, NIV

God's Household

Father God,

I thank you right now for your sons and daughters who have…

- ◆ comforted me when I was hurting,
- ◆ provided support when I was weak,
- ◆ confronted me when I was drifting spiritually,
- ◆ given me confidence when I didn't believe in myself,
- ◆ offered me friendship when I was lonely,
- ◆ shown me truth when I was confused,
- ◆ prayed with me when I faced problems,
- ◆ counseled me when I needed direction.

I am so privileged to be a member of your incredible household.

Look! Here I stand at the door and knock. If you hear me calling and open the door, I will come in, and we will share a meal as friends.

Revelation 3:20, NLT

Your Friend

Lord,

I stand in awe when I consider that you invite me to come before you as a friend. Why would you, the creator of the universe, show me such favor?

I will always speak your name with respect and reverence. I will always proclaim how great and mighty you are. I will always acknowledge that all good gifts are from you. I will always remember that I was created to serve you and to bring you pleasure.

Thank you so much for considering me your friend and for allowing me to see you as the greatest, truest, most compassionate friend a person could ever have.

I STAND IN AWE

I have fought a good fight,

I have finished the race,

and I have remained faithful.

2 Timothy 4:7, NLT

Finishing the Race

Dear God,

I want to love and serve you with passion and commitment all the days of my life. I don't want to merely start a good race and then fall away; I want to successfully complete my lifelong spiritual journey.

I pray for refreshment when my spiritual muscles are weary. I pray for a second wind when I get discouraged. When I lose focus, I pray for a vision of the reward that awaits me at the finish line. I pray for encouragement from other runners when I am tempted to give less than my best or even quit.

On my final day of earthly life, I look forward to seeing you face-to-face and knowing that I have been your faithful and loving servant.

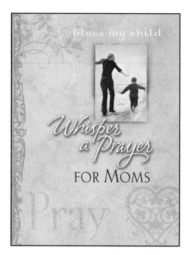

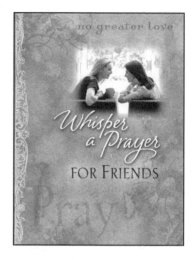

Also from Tyndale House Publishers:

Whisper a Prayer for Moms (0-8423-8295-X)

Whisper a Prayer for Friends (0-8423-8296-8)

Available at your favorite local retailer.